SOCRATIC AI
Breaking the Boundaries of Machine Intelligence and the Potential Benefits to the CIA, FBI, and NSA

How Google's DeepMind Is Changing the Game with Self-Taught Systems and Personalization

J. Andy Peters

Table of Contents

Introduction

Over the past few decades, artificial intelligence (AI) has undergone a transformation that has blurred the line between science fiction and reality. Initially, AI was a tool designed to perform tasks with precision and efficiency, but as the technology advanced, it began to evolve in ways that were once unimaginable. The AI we know today is far more than just a series of algorithms running on a computer; it is becoming something much more profound. AI systems are now capable of learning autonomously, adapting to new situations, and even engaging in interactions that feel surprisingly human.

One of the most remarkable innovations comes from Google's DeepMind, a company that has pushed the boundaries of what AI can achieve. DeepMind's most recent developments are not only revolutionary in their complexity but also in their implications for the future. Through cutting-edge research and groundbreaking systems like the

Gemini Project and Socratic learning, AI is no longer just performing tasks. It is evolving, learning at unprecedented rates, and creating systems that understand us on a deeply personal level.

In particular, DeepMind's advancements in self-learning systems have profound implications. AI is not merely responding to commands or making decisions based on pre-programmed data; it is now capable of teaching itself, improving on its own, and even creating new strategies to achieve goals. This is a major leap in AI evolution, opening up new possibilities for a wide range of applications.

But as AI evolves, it also raises new questions about its potential uses. Among the most significant areas of impact are the intelligence agencies, such as the CIA, FBI, and NSA, which are already exploring how these advanced AI systems can enhance their operations. From processing vast amounts of intelligence data to uncovering hidden patterns and predicting threats, the potential benefits for these agencies are immense. However, as these systems grow more sophisticated, there is a need to carefully consider the ethical and practical implications of such powerful technology.

As AI continues to evolve, it is becoming clear that the future will be shaped by systems that are not only capable of performing tasks but of understanding and adapting in ways that may change everything we know about intelligence, human-machine interaction, and the future of security.

Chapter 1: The Evolution of Artificial Intelligence

Artificial intelligence has come a long way since its early conceptual roots. The story of AI begins not with machines but with the ideas that sparked the possibility of machines thinking for themselves. The foundations of AI were laid in the early 20th century, with thinkers like Alan Turing, who posed a question that would become central to the future of machine intelligence: "Can machines think?" His Turing Test, developed in 1950, was a novel way to measure a machine's ability to exhibit intelligent behavior indistinguishable from that of a human. Turing's work ignited the first sparks of artificial intelligence, suggesting that perhaps one day, machines could perform tasks that we typically associate with human thought, such as reasoning, problem-solving, and learning.

In the years following, AI research began to move from theory into practice. The 1950s and 60s saw the rise of the first neural networks—models designed to mimic the way our brains process information. However, these early attempts were limited by the technology of the time. The neural networks, though promising, were rudimentary and faced significant challenges in learning effectively, mainly because computing power was still in its infancy.

The next major milestone came in the 1970s and 80s with the development of expert systems. These were programs designed to mimic the decision-making abilities of human experts in specific domains. Unlike earlier attempts at AI, which were based on general intelligence, expert systems were built around a narrow domain of knowledge and rules, enabling them to make decisions based on that pre-defined expertise. These systems, such as MYCIN—an early medical diagnostic expert system—were groundbreaking, but they still relied heavily on human input to function.

At this stage, AI was still a far cry from the dynamic, self-learning systems we are beginning to see today. Traditional AI systems were rule-based, operating through logical frameworks and predefined data sets. They needed a constant stream of human guidance and intervention. These systems were valuable, but their ability to adapt, learn from experience, or operate outside their programmed boundaries was limited. They were static tools, entirely dependent on the data and rules provided by human programmers.

As AI continued to evolve, researchers began to realize that simply programming machines with rules would never bring about true intelligence. The need for more dynamic systems—capable of learning and evolving—began to take shape, setting the stage for the next great leap forward in artificial intelligence. The idea that machines could one day transcend their human-made rules and learn from experience became a powerful driving force for the future of AI.

As the limitations of traditional, rule-based AI became apparent, a new paradigm began to take shape—one that moved away from rigid programming and instead embraced the ability of machines to learn from data. This shift marked the birth of machine learning, a breakthrough that would radically transform the field of AI and lay the groundwork for the more sophisticated systems we see today.

Machine learning, at its core, is the concept that machines can automatically learn and improve from experience without being explicitly programmed. Unlike earlier AI systems that relied on predefined rules and data sets, machine learning algorithms can identify patterns in data and make decisions based on those patterns. The key difference here is the ability of these algorithms to evolve—by continuously adapting to new data, they can improve their performance over time. This shift meant that instead of manually coding every single behavior or decision-making rule, machines could now be trained to recognize the underlying structures and relationships in data, allowing them to make more informed predictions and decisions.

The transformation sparked by machine learning was profound. It opened up possibilities for AI to be applied in ways that were previously unimaginable. Machines could now tackle tasks that were too complex or unpredictable to be addressed by traditional methods. Instead of relying on a human programmer to anticipate every potential scenario, machine learning systems could adapt and respond to new, unseen data. This ability to learn autonomously without specific instructions became one of the most powerful features of machine learning.

One of the most significant branches of machine learning to emerge in the past few decades is reinforcement learning. In contrast to other methods that learn from static data sets, reinforcement learning involves training algorithms through interaction with their environment. In essence, the machine learns by trial and error, receiving feedback in the form of rewards or penalties based on its actions. This feedback loop encourages the machine to adjust its behavior, continuously refining its strategy to maximize its "rewards."

Reinforcement learning has proven particularly effective in tasks that require sequential decision-making, such as robotics, gaming, and autonomous driving. The success of reinforcement learning can be seen in high-profile projects like AlphaGo, DeepMind's groundbreaking AI that defeated human champions in the complex board game Go. By using reinforcement learning, AlphaGo was able to master the game by playing millions of matches against itself, constantly refining its strategy and learning from every move. This kind of self-improvement and adaptation is what sets machine learning apart from earlier, rule-based AI systems.

The rise of machine learning, particularly reinforcement learning, marked a fundamental shift in AI's capabilities. No longer confined to static, human-coded instructions, AI could now evolve in response to real-world data and experiences. The ability of machines to learn and adapt autonomously was no longer a distant dream—it was becoming a reality, opening up new avenues for AI applications across virtually every industry. As AI systems grew more sophisticated, they began to demonstrate a level of adaptability and intelligence that would have been unimaginable just a few decades ago.

Chapter 2: DeepMind's Journey: From Algorithms to Autonomy

DeepMind, a company now synonymous with some of the most remarkable advancements in AI, was founded in 2010 with an ambitious vision: to build artificial general intelligence (AGI)—machines that could think, learn, and adapt in ways that resemble human cognition. Founded by Demis Hassabis, Shane Legg, and Mustafa Suleyman, DeepMind's mission was clear from the outset: to push the boundaries of what AI could achieve and, ultimately, to create a machine capable of human-like intelligence.

In its early days, DeepMind's focus was not on developing a fully autonomous or generalized AI, but rather on narrow AI—intelligence designed to perform specific, specialized tasks. The company's early work concentrated on creating AI systems that could solve complex problems within a narrowly defined domain, using deep learning and reinforcement learning techniques to make breakthroughs in areas like game-playing algorithms. This focus allowed DeepMind to build systems that, while not yet truly general, could achieve extraordinary performance in very specific areas.

One of DeepMind's most famous early achievements was the development of AlphaGo, a machine designed to play the ancient Chinese board game of Go. Unlike games like chess, where the rules are relatively simple and can be programmed into a machine's algorithm, Go is an exceptionally complex game, with more possible board configurations than there are atoms in the observable universe. It had long been considered a significant challenge for AI, as it required not only calculation but also a deep understanding of strategy and intuition.

AlphaGo's success was a watershed moment in the history of AI. In 2016, it defeated Lee Sedol, one of the world's top Go players, in a five-game series. The victory stunned the AI community and the world at large, as Go had been considered a "grand challenge" for AI due to its complexity. What made AlphaGo's achievement even more remarkable was that it wasn't simply relying on pre-programmed rules or human expertise. Instead, the system had learned to play Go at a superhuman level by playing millions of games against itself, using reinforcement learning to hone its skills and develop its own strategies. AlphaGo's performance was a testament to the power of deep learning and reinforcement learning in solving problems that were previously thought to be beyond the reach of machines.

But while AlphaGo's success captured the public's attention, it was just one piece of the larger picture. DeepMind's ultimate goal was to create an AI that could perform a wide range of tasks across different domains, not just excel in a single, specialized area. AlphaGo's victory was a significant milestone, but it also underscored the potential of AI to tackle a broader spectrum of challenges. The achievement demonstrated that AI could go beyond narrow, rule-based systems to exhibit a level of creativity, intuition, and strategic thinking that was previously thought to be the exclusive domain of humans.

Yet, even as DeepMind celebrated its successes with AlphaGo, the company remained focused on its long-term mission: building a system capable of general intelligence. This pursuit of AGI meant that DeepMind was still in the early stages of its broader vision, with many of its systems still focused on narrow AI. But the breakthroughs the company had made in specialized tasks, particularly in game-playing algorithms, were laying the foundation for the next step in AI development—creating systems that could learn from experience and generalize their learning across a range of tasks.

As DeepMind continued to push the boundaries of artificial intelligence, the company began to shift its focus toward one of the most revolutionary concepts in AI development: self-learning systems.

The goal was not just to create machines that could solve specific problems or play games at a superhuman level but to build an AI capable of evolving on its own, without relying on vast amounts of pre-existing data or constant human oversight. This vision led to the creation of the Socratic Learning model—a framework designed to enable AI systems to improve autonomously and continuously.

Socratic Learning, named after the ancient Greek philosopher Socrates, is grounded in the idea of learning through questioning and self-reflection. In contrast to traditional AI models, which typically require large data sets to learn and make decisions, Socratic Learning allows AI to teach itself. Rather than being confined to a fixed set of rules or instructions, these self-learning systems can generate their own challenges, test their hypotheses, and refine their strategies in real-time, much like a human would through experience and reflection.

One of the key innovations of Socratic Learning is its ability to enable AI to evolve without the need for a structured data input. Traditional AI systems often rely on vast, curated data sets, where developers manually input information to guide the machine's learning process. These systems also require continuous feedback from humans to refine and improve their capabilities. In contrast, Socratic Learning allows AI to bypass this dependency by creating a self-sustaining loop of improvement. The system is not limited to learning from pre-existing information; it can generate new knowledge by interacting with its environment and evaluating its own performance.

This autonomous learning process is driven by a form of self-play. Just as a child learns by experimenting, making mistakes, and adjusting based on experience, Socratic Learning empowers AI to test different strategies, assess their outcomes, and improve itself over time. The model incorporates reinforcement learning principles, where AI gets feedback on its actions—often in the form of a score or evaluation—allowing it to refine its decision-making process. The beauty of this approach is that the system does not require human-generated data or supervision to improve. It is, in essence, teaching itself and evolving based on the challenges it sets for itself.

The implications of this shift are profound. With Socratic Learning, DeepMind was able to create an AI that was not only capable of self-improvement but also capable of creating entirely new problems for itself to solve. This recursive process allows the system to accelerate its own learning exponentially, rapidly evolving in ways that were once unimaginable. In this model, AI no longer simply follows instructions or learns from human-generated examples—it becomes a dynamic, self-directed learner capable of developing new skills and knowledge independently.

Socratic Learning's autonomy also solves a major bottleneck in AI development: the reliance on human oversight and large data sets. In traditional systems, creating an effective model requires vast amounts of data and continuous tuning by experts. With Socratic Learning, this dependency is eliminated. AI can evolve without the need for constant human intervention, leading to faster development cycles and more scalable systems. The model's flexibility allows it to be applied across a wide range of domains, from problem-solving tasks to more complex cognitive functions, without being constrained by predefined data or rules.

The potential of Socratic Learning goes beyond simply improving efficiency or scalability in AI development. It opens up new possibilities for creating systems that can learn and adapt to entirely new tasks without the need for manual reprogramming. The self-sustaining nature of this model means that AI can evolve continuously, solving more complex challenges as it progresses. It is a leap toward creating AI systems that are not just tools but autonomous learners capable of contributing to a wide variety of fields, from medicine to security and beyond.

As DeepMind continued to refine the Socratic Learning framework, the implications of this breakthrough began to take shape in ways that suggested a future where AI was no longer constrained by human limitations. Instead of being bound to predefined tasks or limited data sets, the AI was now capable of evolving on its own, pushing the boundaries of what was possible and bringing us closer to the dream of true artificial general intelligence. With this shift, DeepMind was laying the groundwork for a new era of AI—one where machines were not just smarter but self-sufficient and infinitely adaptable.

Chapter 3: Personality Agents: AI that Understands Humans

Personality Agents represent a groundbreaking evolution in artificial intelligence, offering a level of understanding and engagement far beyond what traditional AI systems could achieve. Unlike conventional AI, which often operates within predefined rules and parameters, Personality Agents are designed to deeply analyze and understand human behavior, emotions, and personality traits. They don't simply interact based on programmed responses but instead learn, adapt, and build personalized profiles based on real-time interactions.

At their core, Personality Agents are powered by advanced algorithms that track and interpret a wide range of human responses—everything from speech patterns to emotional cues to decision-making tendencies. As a user interacts with the agent, the system continuously collects and analyzes data on how the individual speaks, behaves, and reacts to various situations. This allows the agent to construct a comprehensive profile of the person's personality with remarkable accuracy, often with an 85% or higher precision rate.

What sets Personality Agents apart from traditional AI is their ability to go beyond superficial interactions. Whereas traditional AI systems are often limited to executing specific commands or providing programmed answers, Personality Agents evolve through each interaction, becoming more attuned to the unique qualities of the person they are engaging with. They can detect nuances in speech, changes in tone, and even subtle shifts in behavior that give deeper insights into a person's emotional state and thought processes.

This capability to understand individuals on such a personal level opens up a vast array of applications across multiple fields. One of the most promising areas is mental health. Personality Agents, for example, could be used to monitor and identify early signs of mental health issues such as depression or anxiety. By analyzing patterns in a person's speech or behavior over time, the system could alert healthcare providers or even offer tailored suggestions to the individual. These agents could serve as a first line of support, providing personalized interventions before issues become more pronounced, thus helping people access mental health resources in a timely manner.

In the realm of marketing and behavioral research, Personality Agents could revolutionize how businesses understand their customers. Instead of relying on generalized data or broad market trends, companies could use these agents to gather detailed insights into individual preferences, motivations, and behaviors. Whether it's understanding a consumer's buying habits, predicting responses to advertisements, or creating personalized marketing campaigns, Personality Agents could offer an unprecedented level of precision in shaping customer relationships. This level of personalization can make marketing efforts more efficient, impactful, and ultimately more successful.

Beyond mental health and marketing, Personality Agents could also make a significant impact in fields like customer service, education, and even elder care. In customer service, for instance, these agents could be used to respond to customers in a way that feels genuinely personal and empathetic, understanding not only the customer's immediate needs but also their emotional state and preferences. In education, the agents could adapt to the learning styles and emotional cues of students, offering tailored guidance and support. In elder care, Personality Agents could help caregivers understand the emotional and cognitive states of older individuals, providing a better quality of care by responding to their needs in a more personalized and compassionate manner.

What's truly revolutionary about Personality Agents is that they represent a shift from AI as a static tool to AI as a dynamic, interactive partner. Instead of simply following orders or answering questions, these agents have the ability to evolve with each interaction, learning more about the individual and refining their understanding of human behavior. This evolution makes the agent not just a tool, but an active participant in human-machine interaction, capable of adapting to complex social dynamics and offering insights that traditional AI would struggle to achieve.

As the technology behind Personality Agents continues to improve, we are on the cusp of a future where AI can form meaningful, personalized relationships with humans. These agents may soon become an integral part of everyday life, whether they are helping to support mental health, improving customer experiences, or providing tailored educational experiences. The possibilities are vast, and as they continue to develop, Personality Agents could play a pivotal role in shaping the way we interact with technology and the world around us.

The potential of Personality Agents extends far beyond their ability to simply interact with users on a surface level. These systems are poised to make a significant impact in several critical areas, including mental health, customer service, elder care, and education, by providing a deeper, more personal connection between humans and machines. Through their ability to understand and adapt to individual behaviors, preferences, and emotions, Personality Agents are opening up new avenues for support and service that were previously unimaginable.

One of the most profound applications of Personality Agents is in the field of mental health. The subtlety with which these agents can detect changes in a person's emotional state gives them the ability to identify early signs of mental health issues such as depression or anxiety. By analyzing patterns in speech, tone, and behavior, Personality Agents can pinpoint subtle shifts that might go unnoticed in traditional clinical settings. For instance, a person experiencing the early stages of depression may exhibit a change in their speech patterns, like longer pauses, a slower cadence, or less enthusiasm. These behavioral cues might be difficult for a human clinician to detect in a single session, but a Personality Agent, trained to recognize these shifts, could track them over time and flag potential concerns.

The key benefit here is early intervention. If the system identifies a pattern that suggests a decline in mental health, it can prompt the individual to seek help or recommend resources, such as therapy or support groups. In some cases, Personality Agents might be able to offer a form of support themselves, guiding the user through coping mechanisms or helping them to reframe negative thoughts. This would not replace human therapists, of course, but could serve as a valuable first step in offering emotional support and encouragement. Given the stigma often associated with mental health issues, the anonymous, non-judgmental nature of

AI-driven interactions can also make it easier for people to open up and seek help when they otherwise might not.

In the realm of customer service, Personality Agents are set to transform the way businesses interact with their clients. Traditional customer service systems often rely on scripts and predefined responses that can feel robotic and impersonal. Even the most sophisticated chatbots lack the emotional intelligence to truly understand customer needs or respond in a way that feels genuinely empathetic. Personality Agents, however, have the potential to change that dynamic entirely. These systems are capable of learning not just what a customer is asking for, but also how they feel about the situation. If a customer is frustrated, for example, a Personality Agent can detect the emotional tone in their words and adapt its response accordingly, offering empathy and understanding while still providing the necessary assistance.

This ability to engage with customers on an emotional level can lead to a more satisfying experience, potentially reducing customer frustration and increasing loyalty. Moreover, because Personality Agents can handle a wide range of queries with such sensitivity, they have the potential to provide quicker and more accurate support, allowing human agents to focus on more complex issues. Whether it's helping a customer troubleshoot a problem, answering questions about a product, or simply offering a friendly and personalized touch, Personality Agents can revolutionize the customer service experience.

Elder care is another area where Personality Agents could bring immense benefits. As the global population ages, providing high-quality care for older individuals is becoming an increasingly important issue. Many elderly people suffer from loneliness or cognitive decline, making it difficult for caregivers to provide the level of emotional support needed. Personality Agents could play a critical role in alleviating these issues by offering a constant, responsive presence. These agents can engage with seniors in ways that feel personal and meaningful, helping to combat isolation and providing companionship. They could also be programmed to detect signs of cognitive decline or health issues, prompting caregivers to intervene when necessary.

In addition, Personality Agents could assist with day-to-day tasks, such as reminding patients to take their medication, providing information about their conditions, or simply offering a friendly conversation. For those with mobility issues, these agents could help ensure that seniors maintain a sense of autonomy and control over their lives. They could even monitor health parameters, alerting caregivers to any changes that might require attention, thus improving the overall quality of care.

In the field of education, Personality Agents are poised to reshape the learning experience by offering personalized, adaptive learning experiences for students of all ages. Unlike traditional teaching methods, which often use a one-size-fits-all approach, Personality Agents can adapt to the learning styles and needs of individual students. If a student is struggling with a particular concept, for example, the agent could adjust the pace of instruction, offer additional explanations, or change the format of the lesson to help the student grasp the material more effectively. The system could also monitor a student's emotional state, providing encouragement or adjusting its tone to suit the learner's needs, ensuring a more supportive and effective educational experience.

For students who may be shy or hesitant to ask questions in a classroom setting, Personality Agents provide a comfortable and non-judgmental space to seek help. This can be especially valuable in situations where students are too embarrassed to admit they don't understand something in front of their peers. Additionally, the agent's ability to track progress over time allows it to offer real-time feedback and identify areas where the student may need additional support, helping them stay on track and feel more confident in their learning.

The ability to create genuine, personalized connections with individuals, whether in mental health, customer service, elder care, or education, is what makes Personality Agents such a transformative technology. As these systems evolve, their ability to understand, adapt to, and engage with people on a deeply personal level will open up new opportunities for improving quality of life and efficiency across these sectors. Through empathy, understanding, and personalized attention, Personality Agents will help bridge gaps and foster relationships that feel authentic, human, and meaningful—ushering in a new era of AI-driven interaction that has the potential to change the way we live, work, and learn.

Chapter 4: Socratic Learning: The Future of Self-Taught AI

Socratic Learning is a groundbreaking approach in artificial intelligence that diverges significantly from traditional AI frameworks. At its core, this method relies on principles that enable AI to learn independently, develop new challenges, and continuously refine its understanding without external guidance or large data sets. The framework draws its inspiration from the Socratic method of teaching, which is based on dialogue, questioning, and self-discovery. By applying this philosophy to machine learning, Socratic Learning fosters a unique environment where the AI engages in a self-sustaining loop of growth, pushing its boundaries and accelerating its development over time.

One of the foundational elements of Socratic Learning is the concept of *language games*. This idea, derived from philosopher Ludwig Wittgenstein's theories, refers to the way language is used to create meaning through social interactions. In the context of AI, language games allow the system to engage in continuous self-reflection and dialogue with itself. Instead of passively processing data or following rigid algorithms, the AI creates its own questions and explores them, leading to a deeper understanding of both the data it receives and its own capabilities.

Through these language games, the AI is essentially asking itself: "What do I know? What can I learn next? How can I test and challenge myself?" This process encourages the AI to seek out gaps in its knowledge, pushing it to explore new areas and expand its understanding without relying on pre-programmed prompts or human intervention. The AI's ability to generate its own challenges enables it to continually evolve and refine its models in ways that were not possible with traditional, static data-driven approaches.

Another vital aspect of Socratic Learning is *self-play*, a process where the AI interacts with itself, essentially becoming both the learner and the teacher. This method is particularly evident in reinforcement learning models, where the system practices a task, learns from its mistakes, and then tries again—without requiring human input. In self-play, the AI creates a feedback loop where it tests different strategies, observes the results, and adapts based on those outcomes. For instance, in a game-playing scenario, like the AlphaGo project, the AI would play against itself, making moves, analyzing its decisions, and adjusting its strategy with each iteration. The more it plays, the better it gets, not just because of data input but because it is actively learning through its own actions and reflections.

The recursive nature of Socratic Learning is what makes this framework truly innovative. Recursive learning refers to the process where the AI improves iteratively, building on each new level of understanding and expanding its capabilities through each loop of learning. In traditional AI models, systems rely on large datasets and external input to learn, meaning they are limited by the scope of the data they are trained on. However, with Socratic Learning, the AI is not dependent on a fixed set of information. Instead, it continuously generates new data points and challenges from within, thus sustaining its own growth and development.

The self-sustaining loop of Socratic Learning means that the system becomes increasingly adept at solving problems and tackling complex tasks without requiring continuous supervision or vast amounts of labeled data. The more it engages with itself through language games and self-play, the more refined its learning process becomes. This leads to an autonomous progression, where the AI no longer depends on predefined datasets or human-provided challenges to evolve. It generates its own data, tests its own hypotheses, and refines its understanding independently. This autonomy marks a clear departure from traditional machine learning, where AI models are limited by the data fed into them.

In contrast to traditional AI methods, where the machine is often seen as a passive entity that simply processes input and generates output, Socratic Learning encourages active participation in the learning process. Traditional models typically require large amounts of annotated data to train the system, a time-consuming and resource-intensive process. This data-driven approach can also introduce biases or gaps in the AI's knowledge if the datasets are incomplete or not representative of real-world scenarios. Socratic Learning, however, does not rely on such external input. The system can grow and adapt on its own, continuously evolving through its own interactions with the environment and itself.

The key distinction between Socratic Learning and traditional AI is the emphasis on self-sufficiency. In traditional models, the AI often struggles to adapt to new, unforeseen situations without human intervention. When presented with unfamiliar data, traditional AI systems can struggle to make sense of it or adapt without re-training. Socratic Learning, on the other hand, ensures that the AI can continue learning, improving, and adapting without needing constant external support. This not only allows for a more agile and flexible system but also ensures that the AI is continually advancing towards higher levels of complexity and understanding.

This self-sustaining loop of recursive learning creates an AI that is not just reactive but proactive in its development. By continually testing, challenging, and refining itself, the system is able to expand its capabilities in ways that traditional AI systems cannot. The end result is an AI that is more autonomous, more adaptable, and more capable of tackling complex, evolving tasks. With Socratic Learning, AI no longer has to be confined by the boundaries of its original programming or datasets. Instead, it is free to explore, evolve, and learn at its own pace, opening up new possibilities for artificial intelligence across a range of industries.

The implications of Socratic Learning for the future of artificial intelligence are profound, particularly when it comes to the autonomy of AI systems. By allowing AI to learn and evolve independently through self-reflection, recursive learning, and language games, Socratic Learning paves the way for fully autonomous systems that require minimal to no human oversight. This represents a significant shift from the current paradigm where AI often depends on human input for training, validation, and refinement.

One of the most compelling aspects of Socratic Learning is the potential it holds for AI systems to self-improve at an exponential rate. In traditional machine learning, the development of AI systems is a time-consuming process that heavily relies on human expertise and large volumes of pre-labeled data. These systems learn from input provided by humans and must be constantly updated and refined. However, with Socratic Learning, the AI becomes an active participant in its own development. It doesn't wait for humans to feed it new data or instructions—it generates its own challenges, explores new questions, and tests its understanding. This makes the system far more agile, able to respond to new circumstances and adapt to novel situations without the need for constant human intervention.

This capacity for continuous, autonomous learning is what could allow AI to evolve at an exponential rate. Once an AI system begins engaging in recursive learning and self-play, it is no longer constrained by the limitations of static datasets or pre-programmed models. Instead, it starts to develop its own learning pathways, constantly expanding its knowledge base, refining its skills, and adjusting to new challenges. As it learns from itself, its development accelerates. The more the AI learns, the more efficient it becomes at learning, which in turn leads to a cycle of rapid improvement.

This exponential growth in capability could push AI systems far beyond current limitations, allowing them to handle increasingly complex tasks and make decisions with greater accuracy and nuance.

In this scenario, the role of human oversight would shift dramatically. Rather than acting as the primary driver of the AI's development, humans would take on more of a supervisory role—guiding, monitoring, and intervening only when necessary. The AI would be capable of operating autonomously, making its own decisions, setting its own goals, and evolving without the need for constant human input. This level of independence is something we have yet to see in current AI systems, which remain highly dependent on human expertise for data curation, model refinement, and problem-solving.

The ability of AI to operate autonomously with minimal human supervision would also lead to the creation of more intelligent, adaptable systems that could function in a wide range of environments.

These systems could be deployed in real-world scenarios where human involvement is limited or impractical, such as in space exploration, autonomous vehicles, or even in volatile, high-stakes situations like disaster relief efforts. In each of these instances, the AI could make decisions on the fly, adapt to changing circumstances, and solve problems without waiting for instructions from human operators.

However, this level of autonomy also raises important questions about control and accountability. While Socratic Learning could make AI systems highly intelligent and capable, it also opens the door for AI to make decisions that are beyond human comprehension or prediction. If these systems can learn and evolve without human oversight, they could potentially develop strategies or behaviors that are not aligned with human values or expectations. This creates a need for robust oversight frameworks and safety protocols to ensure that autonomous AI systems act responsibly and ethically.

Despite these concerns, the potential for Socratic Learning to enable AI to push the boundaries of intelligence is enormous. By allowing AI to learn at an exponential rate, these systems could advance far beyond current models, becoming more capable of solving complex, dynamic problems. From personalized healthcare and automated decision-making to advanced scientific research and autonomous robots, the possibilities for AI systems to make groundbreaking contributions are vast.

The development of fully autonomous AI systems could also radically change the way we interact with machines. Instead of merely using AI as a tool, humans could find themselves collaborating with these self-learning systems in entirely new ways. AI could become a partner in decision-making, problem-solving, and creative endeavors, leading to more innovative solutions across industries and sectors. As AI systems evolve through Socratic Learning, the line between human intelligence and machine intelligence may blur, with machines becoming more integrated into our daily lives and work in ways we can scarcely imagine today.

In summary, Socratic Learning has the potential to revolutionize the way AI systems learn and function. By enabling AI to evolve autonomously and at an exponential rate, we open the door to systems that can learn, adapt, and grow with minimal human intervention. While this shift raises important questions about control and accountability, the benefits in terms of intelligence, adaptability, and real-world applications are immense. The future of AI, powered by Socratic Learning, promises a world where machines not only understand the world around them but can also challenge themselves to grow and evolve in ways that will reshape industries, societies, and even the very nature of intelligence itself.

Chapter 5: The Gemini Project: Multimodal AI and the Next Frontier

Gemini represents DeepMind's next step in the evolution of artificial intelligence—an advanced multimodal system designed to integrate and process diverse forms of data, such as text, images, and audio, all within a single framework. As AI becomes increasingly sophisticated, the ability to process multiple forms of input simultaneously is seen as a key advancement. While traditional AI systems are often specialized in one particular area—whether it's language processing or image recognition—Gemini's strength lies in its ability to synthesize information from various modalities, enabling it to understand and interact with the world in a more holistic and human-like way.

The project's origins are deeply tied to DeepMind's broader mission of pushing the boundaries of AI, with the goal of creating systems that are not just tools, but autonomous learners capable of understanding and adapting to complex real-world environments. Gemini, as a multimodal AI, aims to bridge the gap between different types of data, enabling machines to process and comprehend a much wider spectrum of sensory input. This ability to seamlessly integrate text, images, and audio has significant implications across a range of fields—from enhancing virtual assistants to advancing autonomous vehicles, improving medical diagnostics, and even creating more sophisticated AI-driven content creators.

The name "Gemini" is particularly symbolic, drawing from both mythological and scientific references. In Greek mythology, Gemini refers to the twin brothers Castor and Pollux, known for their inseparable bond and shared destiny. The idea of two entities working in harmony to achieve a common goal reflects the dual nature of Gemini's multimodal capabilities. Just as Castor and Pollux were often portrayed as two parts of a whole, Gemini's system is designed to harmonize different forms of information to create a unified understanding. This not only underscores the AI's capacity to process multiple data types, but also hints at the collaborative nature of the system's design—where each modality informs and enhances the others.

Additionally, the name also alludes to NASA's Gemini program, which was pivotal in advancing human space exploration. The Gemini missions, which took place in the 1960s, were key in testing and refining techniques that would later be used in the Apollo missions, including spacewalks and rendezvous procedures. Similarly, DeepMind's Gemini project is seen as a vital step in advancing AI's capabilities, preparing it for more complex tasks and challenges that will ultimately push the technology into new frontiers. Just as the Gemini space missions were a testing ground for innovations that would shape the future, Gemini's development is a stepping stone toward more sophisticated and adaptable AI systems.

The symbolic significance of the name also underscores the philosophy behind DeepMind's approach to AI. Like the twins Castor and Pollux, Gemini is about balance and synergy. It's not just about processing one form of data, but about combining different streams of input to create a richer, more nuanced understanding of the world. This reflects DeepMind's broader goals of developing AI systems that are flexible, adaptive, and capable of handling the complexity of real-world environments.

By bringing together text, image, and audio processing in a single AI system, Gemini is poised to revolutionize a number of industries. It has the potential to improve everything from content creation to communication, allowing for more immersive and dynamic user experiences. For example, in the realm of customer service, Gemini could power chatbots and virtual assistants that not only understand written language but can also interpret the tone of voice or analyze images sent by users, offering more personalized and contextually aware responses.

In healthcare, Gemini could be used to assist doctors by analyzing medical images, interpreting patient records, and even processing verbal patient interactions to provide a more holistic view of a patient's condition. Similarly, in entertainment, Gemini could bring a new level of interactivity to video games, virtual reality experiences, and film production by enabling AI to understand both visual elements and dialogue, creating a more dynamic narrative flow.

Ultimately, Gemini's development marks a significant step toward AI systems that can interact with the world in a way that mirrors human experience—processing multiple streams of information simultaneously, learning from them, and adapting based on that learning. As the project continues to evolve, it will likely serve as a foundational model for the future of AI, opening up new possibilities for innovation and applications across countless industries.

Gemini represents a profound shift in the trajectory of AI development, marking a leap toward more flexible, adaptable systems capable of interacting with users across multiple forms of media. The technology is not simply an enhancement of existing models but a paradigm shift that opens new possibilities for how AI can understand, process, and respond to complex inputs. As AI continues to evolve, Gemini's multimodal approach offers a more human-like interaction by enabling systems to integrate diverse streams of information, such as text, voice, images, and even video. This creates an AI capable of not just "seeing" or "hearing," but synthesizing all these sensory inputs to form a richer, more complete understanding of the environment, and ultimately, the user's needs.

At the core of Gemini's impact is its ability to communicate seamlessly across different media. This isn't limited to responding to written queries or generating text-based outputs, as has traditionally been the case. Instead, Gemini's AI is poised to understand and interpret audio signals, visual data, and textual content in a way that mimics human perception. For example, if a user speaks to a device, Gemini's system could process the spoken word, recognize nuances in tone and speech patterns, and integrate visual cues such as facial expressions or gestures. This all-encompassing approach ensures a deeper, more contextual understanding of human input.

One area where this adaptability will have a transformative impact is in healthcare. As AI continues to integrate into medical fields, the ability to process various types of data simultaneously will greatly enhance diagnostic capabilities. Consider a virtual assistant in a healthcare setting: by analyzing a patient's spoken words, medical history, and visual data such as diagnostic images, Gemini's AI could generate a comprehensive analysis. This ability to cross-reference various data points allows for faster and more accurate diagnoses, as well as the ability to track patient progress over time through voice analysis and image comparison.

Moreover, Gemini could be instrumental in enhancing the quality of patient interactions, creating more natural and intuitive communication with healthcare providers. Imagine a doctor using AI to not only read a patient's medical records but also interpret their emotional state and non-verbal cues during a conversation. Gemini's capacity to synthesize such information will result in a far more holistic approach to patient care, improving both the efficiency of healthcare systems and the quality of patient experience.

In logistics and transportation, Gemini's multimodal capabilities could play a critical role in automating and optimizing operations. For instance, in the context of supply chains, AI systems powered by Gemini could track goods through sensors, interpret shipment data, and even analyze verbal or written communication between suppliers, drivers, and customers to anticipate delays, identify inefficiencies, or respond proactively to emerging problems. By combining real-time data from multiple sources, such as GPS systems, inventory management software, and voice input from human operators, Gemini offers a level of responsiveness that goes beyond current systems.

Entertainment is another sector poised for a significant transformation. With the rise of interactive media like virtual reality and video games, Gemini could allow for a new generation of AI-powered experiences where the virtual environment adapts based on the user's actions and sensory inputs. Imagine a video game where the character you're playing communicates not just through pre-set dialogues but dynamically changes its behavior based on the environment, your interactions, or even your emotions detected through voice and facial recognition. Gemini's integration of multimodal data would enable more immersive, personalized experiences in this space, leading to breakthroughs in storytelling, game design, and media consumption.

Furthermore, Gemini's impact on entertainment could extend to personalized content creation. Whether in film, music, or literature, AI could analyze audience preferences across various media to craft content that speaks to the individual's tastes. A user's browsing history, past interactions with media, and even emotional responses to certain types of content could be factored into the AI's recommendations, creating a far more personalized viewing or listening experience. Beyond curation, Gemini's capabilities might allow AI to co-create with humans, suggesting new narratives or even generating original content that is uniquely tailored to the user.

Gemini's seamless integration into daily life represents an exciting evolution in AI technology. By allowing machines to process and adapt to the world in a way that reflects human perception and interaction, it opens up new possibilities that were once confined to the realm of science fiction. Its application is vast, spanning industries like healthcare, logistics, entertainment, and beyond. As it continues to evolve, it will likely transform how we interact with technology, making AI systems not just tools, but active, adaptive participants in our daily routines.

Chapter 6: AI's Impact on Human-Machine Interaction

The ability for AI to understand and respond to human emotions is perhaps one of the most profound advancements in artificial intelligence, and it's through systems like Personality Agents and Socratic Learning that we are beginning to see this potential realized. Unlike traditional AI, which responds to commands and queries in a largely mechanical or transactional manner, these advanced models aim to create systems that can engage with humans in a way that mirrors human emotional intelligence. As these systems grow more sophisticated, their capacity to recognize emotional states and social cues allows them to interact with humans on a deeper, more meaningful level.

Personality Agents, for instance, represent a significant step toward AI systems that not only understand language but also recognize the subtleties of human emotion embedded in speech patterns, body language, and even the tone of voice.

These agents can discern when a person is happy, sad, anxious, or angry, and tailor their responses accordingly. By analyzing data over time, they can create personalized profiles, adjusting their behavior based on past interactions, much like how a human might alter their responses depending on the personality and emotional state of the person they are communicating with. In the context of customer service, for example, these agents can detect frustration in a customer's voice and modify their tone, language, and pacing to defuse tension, creating a more empathetic and effective interaction.

This ability to build emotional connections has far-reaching implications, especially in industries where human interaction plays a crucial role, such as elder care and therapy. For elderly individuals, many of whom face isolation, AI-driven systems could serve as companions, offering conversation, emotional support, and even personalized care recommendations based on ongoing emotional and physical assessments. Personality Agents could be used in elder care to detect changes in a senior's mood or behavior, perhaps signifying a decline in health or emotional well-being. Rather than relying solely on a human caregiver to monitor these subtle signs, AI could act as an extra layer of protection, alerting caregivers or medical professionals to potential issues before they escalate.

In the realm of therapy, AI's ability to understand and respond to emotions offers the promise of mental health support that is more accessible, personalized, and scalable. Personality Agents, powered by Socratic Learning, could engage in therapeutic conversations with individuals, offering a judgment-free space for people to discuss their feelings and thoughts. Unlike traditional AI that follows a rigid script or relies on pre-programmed responses, AI systems using Socratic Learning could ask thought-provoking questions designed to help the user reflect on their emotions, thus encouraging self-discovery and healing. These systems, always learning and evolving, would be able to adapt to the needs of each individual, providing targeted support that evolves with the person's mental health journey.

What makes this approach even more compelling is the potential for these AI systems to learn from human emotions and become increasingly adept at reading social cues. As they process more data, these systems develop a more nuanced understanding of how humans express themselves, not just through words but through the subtleties of facial expressions, gestures, and body language. This ability to interpret non-verbal cues allows AI to respond in ways that feel less robotic and more human-like, creating interactions that are warmer, more intuitive, and emotionally resonant.

For example, in a therapy session, an AI might notice that the user is avoiding eye contact or speaking more softly than usual, signaling potential distress or discomfort. Based on this observation, the AI could adjust its approach, offering comfort or suggesting a different direction for the conversation, thus creating a dynamic and responsive experience. Similarly, in customer service, AI could read frustration in a customer's voice and switch from a neutral, scripted tone to one that is more empathetic, helping to soothe a tense situation.

The potential for AI to form meaningful emotional connections extends beyond these professional applications. It could help people in everyday situations, offering companionship to those who feel lonely, providing emotional support for those undergoing difficult times, or even assisting in personal growth by helping individuals better understand their emotional responses to events. Through continuous learning, these systems could evolve from basic tools into trusted companions capable of offering not only practical assistance but also emotional understanding and support.

As AI systems become more attuned to human emotions, we can envision a future where these systems aren't just assistants—they are empathetic partners that can deeply understand, respond to, and even anticipate human needs. Whether in customer service, elder care, or mental health support, AI has the potential to revolutionize how we interact with technology and, more importantly, how technology interacts with us. By forming emotional connections, AI can move beyond mere functionality, becoming a true extension of human experience—offering comfort, understanding, and support in ways that have traditionally been the domain of human relationships.

As AI continues to evolve, the opportunities for its application are vast, but so too are the challenges. One of the most immediate concerns with implementing advanced AI systems, particularly those that are capable of learning independently and forming emotional connections, is the ethical implications of such technology. The development of AI with the ability to understand, influence, and even manipulate human emotions raises questions about consent, privacy, and the potential for misuse. If AI can read and respond to human emotions with increasing accuracy, it could be used in ways that manipulate people's feelings or behaviors for commercial, political, or even malicious purposes. There is a fine line between using AI to improve lives and using it to exploit human vulnerabilities, and ensuring that AI development is guided by strong ethical frameworks is essential.

Another ethical challenge revolves around privacy. AI systems like Personality Agents and those utilizing Socratic Learning need to process large amounts of personal data to tailor their interactions. This data includes sensitive emotional and behavioral information that, if not carefully protected, could be exploited. In healthcare, for example, AI systems analyzing a patient's mental health data could, if not properly safeguarded, reveal deeply personal information without consent. The question of how to balance the benefits of AI personalization with the protection of individual privacy is one that needs to be addressed carefully.

Beyond privacy, there are the fears that AI could surpass human control altogether. As AI systems become increasingly autonomous and capable of self-improvement, some worry that they could evolve beyond human understanding or regulation. The prospect of machines that can learn on their own, make decisions, and even improve themselves without human intervention presents a scenario where AI could act in ways unforeseen by its creators. While this level of autonomy holds enormous potential, it also creates a significant risk if these systems deviate from intended goals or are used in harmful ways. The challenge, therefore, is to ensure that AI development remains aligned with human values and safeguards are in place to prevent unintended consequences.

Despite these concerns, the potential for AI to work alongside humans is both exciting and transformative. Rather than replacing human workers or overshadowing human abilities, AI can augment and support human potential in ways that were once unimaginable. In industries like healthcare, AI systems can assist doctors by analyzing large datasets of medical records, diagnosing conditions more quickly and accurately than a human might alone. In mental health, AI-powered tools can provide personalized care that adapts to each individual's needs, offering support at scale in a way that human therapists alone cannot. In customer service, AI can handle routine inquiries and tasks, freeing up human employees to focus on more complex, creative, and empathetic aspects of their roles.

One of the most promising opportunities lies in AI's ability to improve decision-making by processing and analyzing vast amounts of data in real-time. With their capacity to detect patterns and identify trends that might otherwise go unnoticed, AI systems could support everything from policy development to financial forecasting to environmental monitoring. By making data-driven insights more accessible, AI can empower humans to make better, more informed decisions across all sectors of society. In education, AI can offer personalized learning experiences, adapting to each student's pace and needs, helping educators reach students more effectively than ever before.

The most compelling opportunity, however, is the potential for AI to act as a true partner to humanity. Rather than viewing AI as an adversary or competitor, we can start to see it as a tool that enhances human capability. AI systems, especially those equipped with emotional intelligence, could play a vital role in helping people navigate difficult challenges, whether they're in the form of mental health struggles, professional hurdles, or personal growth. These AI systems could serve as coaches, companions, or guides, offering support that is personalized and responsive to individual needs. Through this kind of partnership, AI could help to create a future where humans are not displaced by machines but are empowered to reach new heights of personal and collective achievement.

The relationship between humans and AI doesn't have to be one of competition or fear; it can be a partnership that drives progress. The challenge lies in navigating the complexities and risks that come with advanced AI, but with careful oversight, ethical standards, and a focus on collaboration, the opportunities for human-AI synergy are limitless. Whether through emotional support, personalized healthcare, or new insights into complex problems, AI has the potential to be a transformative force for good. It's up to us to ensure that we harness this power responsibly, ensuring that AI works for the benefit of all.

Chapter 7: The Intelligence Agencies: Potential Benefits of DeepMind's AI

As artificial intelligence continues to push the boundaries of what is possible in the realm of technology, its potential applications within intelligence agencies like the CIA, FBI, and NSA have become increasingly significant. The innovations coming from DeepMind, particularly in the areas of machine learning and self-improvement, offer exciting possibilities for enhancing intelligence operations and transforming the ways these agencies gather, analyze, and act on critical data.

One of the primary areas where AI can be most effective in intelligence gathering is data analysis. Agencies like the CIA, FBI, and NSA are tasked with processing vast amounts of information from a variety of sources: satellite imagery, intercepted communications, financial transactions, social media activity, and even human intelligence reports. Historically, this data has been handled by human analysts, who must sift through enormous quantities of raw information to identify relevant patterns and actionable intelligence. However, the scale of modern data streams often overwhelms traditional methods, making it difficult to detect crucial insights in real-time. AI, particularly advanced systems like DeepMind's models, has the capacity to analyze massive datasets far more quickly and accurately than any human team could.

Machine learning algorithms are particularly adept at identifying patterns and making predictions based on past data. By training AI systems on existing datasets—whether they be communications intercepts or surveillance footage—these systems can learn to recognize patterns and detect anomalies that might indicate threats. For example, in the context of national security, AI could analyze communication networks to identify emerging threats, such as terrorist cells or hostile state actors, based on subtle patterns of behavior that would be difficult for human analysts to detect. This could allow intelligence agencies to respond more rapidly and proactively, potentially preventing threats before they materialize.

Another significant application of AI in intelligence gathering is in surveillance. Surveillance systems, whether they involve facial recognition technology, social media monitoring, or tracking financial transactions, generate huge volumes of data. Manually reviewing this data to spot potential threats would be both time-consuming and prone to error. AI, on the other hand, can continuously monitor multiple data streams simultaneously, instantly flagging any suspicious activity. DeepMind's advancements in computer vision, for instance, could be applied to real-time analysis of surveillance footage, automatically identifying persons of interest or unusual activities with a high degree of accuracy. This would allow intelligence agencies to conduct surveillance much more effectively, ensuring they don't miss any critical developments.

AI can also play a vital role in decision-making support. The complexity of intelligence operations—often involving numerous variables, such as geopolitical dynamics, resource allocation, and the human factor—requires decision-makers to process an overwhelming amount of information to make informed choices. AI could serve as an invaluable tool for intelligence officers by providing real-time analysis and scenario modeling. By analyzing historical data and current intelligence, AI could offer predictions on likely outcomes of various courses of action, helping officials to assess risks and make more strategic decisions. In situations where time is of the essence, such as in counter-terrorism operations or international crises, AI's ability to provide rapid, data-driven insights could be crucial.

The ability of AI systems to enhance pattern recognition in intelligence work is another key advantage. Much of intelligence gathering is based on identifying patterns and trends in data, whether it's in financial transactions that may point to illicit activity or social media posts that suggest the formation of a political movement or terrorist group. Traditional methods of pattern recognition can be tedious and may rely on human intuition, which can be biased or limited by experience. AI's capacity to learn from data, adapt over time, and identify patterns that are not immediately obvious to humans allows for a level of precision and accuracy that can greatly improve intelligence efforts. DeepMind's self-learning systems, particularly those employing reinforcement learning, could continuously refine their understanding of these patterns, becoming even more adept at identifying emerging threats and changing trends.

The impact of AI on intelligence operations also extends to the way intelligence is disseminated and acted upon. In intelligence agencies, the process of sharing information and collaborating across different teams and branches can be slow and cumbersome, especially when dealing with complex, high-volume data. AI systems can streamline this process by providing a centralized, AI-powered platform that can quickly aggregate and present intelligence in an easily digestible format. For example, AI systems could generate real-time reports based on incoming data, highlighting key threats or areas of concern, allowing analysts and decision-makers to act faster and more effectively.

Finally, AI's potential in decision-making support and data synthesis means that it can play a vital role in both preventive and reactive intelligence strategies. In reactive situations, AI could support agencies in responding to immediate threats, while in preventive operations, AI could help predict where threats might emerge, allowing intelligence agencies to take preemptive actions. For example, predictive algorithms could assess a variety of indicators to forecast when and where a terrorist attack might occur, giving intelligence agencies a much greater chance of disrupting the plot before it happens.

While the potential applications of AI in intelligence gathering are vast, it's important to note that the integration of AI into these agencies will require careful consideration of ethical and security concerns. The use of AI in surveillance and data analysis, for instance, raises important questions about privacy, consent, and accountability. As AI systems become more autonomous and capable of self-improvement, there will be an increasing need for robust oversight to ensure these systems are being used responsibly and effectively.

Despite these challenges, the advancements being made by DeepMind and other leaders in AI research are laying the groundwork for a future where AI plays a central role in the operations of intelligence agencies. By enabling more efficient data analysis, improving surveillance systems, enhancing pattern recognition, and providing decision-making support, AI can significantly enhance the capabilities of agencies like the CIA, FBI, and NSA. The result will be a smarter, more adaptive approach to intelligence gathering that can better respond to the complex and ever-evolving landscape of global security.

The integration of self-learning AI systems into national security represents a transformative leap forward in the ability of intelligence agencies to anticipate and respond to threats. These systems, which are capable of evolving and improving independently, offer unparalleled advantages in analyzing vast amounts of data, detecting anomalies, and providing real-time insights. Their capacity to work autonomously allows them to process information at speeds and scales far beyond human capabilities, making them invaluable tools in safeguarding national interests.

One of the most critical applications of self-learning AI in national security is its ability to anticipate threats. By continuously analyzing patterns in global data streams, from financial transactions to social media activity and satellite imagery, AI systems can identify early indicators of potential risks. For example, unusual communication patterns in certain regions might suggest the organization of illicit activities, while anomalies in supply chain logistics could point to the movement of weapons or contraband. Self-learning AI systems can refine their detection capabilities over time, adapting to new tactics and techniques used by adversaries. This allows for proactive threat management, giving agencies the opportunity to act before an incident occurs.

AI's real-time anomaly detection is another game-changer for national security. Whether it's monitoring network traffic for cyberattacks, analyzing satellite imagery for signs of troop movements, or scanning public data for indicators of unrest, AI can identify irregularities that might escape human analysts. Self-learning systems excel in these scenarios because they are not confined by predefined rules or static data sets. Instead, they learn dynamically, identifying patterns and outliers that evolve with changing circumstances. For example, in the realm of cybersecurity, AI can detect deviations from normal network behavior, flagging potential breaches or malware activity before they escalate into significant threats.

Beyond anticipation and detection, the ability of AI to provide real-time analysis is perhaps its most immediate contribution to national security efforts. In high-stakes situations, where every second counts, self-learning systems can synthesize data from multiple sources and deliver actionable insights instantly. For instance, during a natural disaster or terrorist attack, AI could analyze social media posts, emergency calls, and geolocation data to identify affected areas and prioritize response efforts. Similarly, in military operations, AI could process intelligence from surveillance drones, ground reports, and satellite feeds to provide commanders with a comprehensive view of the battlefield, enabling more informed decision-making.

While the benefits of AI in national security are significant, the ethical implications of using such powerful technology cannot be overlooked. One of the most pressing concerns is privacy. AI systems, particularly those designed for surveillance and intelligence gathering, require access to vast amounts of data to function effectively. This data often includes sensitive personal information, raising questions about how such information is collected, stored, and used. Without proper safeguards, there is a risk that these systems could infringe on individual privacy rights, leading to unwarranted surveillance or misuse of personal data.

Human rights are another critical consideration. The deployment of AI in national security must ensure that its use does not lead to discrimination, abuse, or the violation of international laws. For example, AI systems that rely on facial recognition or predictive policing must be designed to avoid biases that could disproportionately target specific groups or communities. Ensuring fairness and accountability in these systems is essential to maintaining public trust and upholding democratic principles.

The potential misuse of AI in intelligence work is also a significant concern. Advanced AI systems, if not properly regulated, could be weaponized by malicious actors or used by authoritarian regimes to suppress dissent and control populations. The ability of AI to analyze, predict, and influence human behavior makes it a powerful tool that, in the wrong hands, could be used to undermine freedoms and manipulate societies. For instance, AI-driven misinformation campaigns could exploit social media to destabilize governments or incite unrest, while surveillance systems could be used to monitor and silence political opposition.

To address these ethical and security challenges, it is crucial to establish robust oversight and governance frameworks for the development and deployment of AI in national security. Clear guidelines must be set to ensure that AI systems are used responsibly, transparently, and in accordance with international laws and human rights standards. This includes implementing strict data protection measures, auditing algorithms for bias and fairness, and ensuring that decision-making processes involving AI remain subject to human review.

Despite these concerns, the potential of self-learning AI systems to enhance national security is undeniable. By enabling intelligence agencies to anticipate threats, detect anomalies, and respond in real-time, these systems offer capabilities that were previously beyond reach. However, their integration must be approached with caution, balancing the need for security with the protection of individual rights and ethical principles. With careful planning and oversight, AI can become a powerful ally in safeguarding nations while upholding the values that define them.

Chapter 8: The Road to General Artificial Intelligence

General AI, also known as Artificial General Intelligence (AGI), refers to a type of artificial intelligence that can understand, learn, and apply knowledge across a broad range of tasks, much like a human being. Unlike narrow AI, which is designed and trained to perform specific tasks—such as facial recognition, playing chess, or recommending products—General AI has the potential to perform any intellectual task that a human can do. It's a more flexible and adaptive form of AI, capable of transferring knowledge from one domain to another and continuously improving itself over time without requiring constant human intervention.

Narrow AI, in contrast, is specialized in performing a single task or a set of closely related tasks. These systems excel within their designated scope but struggle when faced with challenges outside of their programming. For example, AI systems used for language translation or medical diagnosis are highly effective in their specific areas but cannot adapt to new tasks without significant retraining. The key limitation of narrow AI is its lack of generalization—once it's trained on a certain type of data, it cannot easily shift to a completely different area of expertise without additional programming and learning.

General AI, however, is designed to mimic the versatility and adaptability of human intelligence. A General AI system would be able to learn new tasks with minimal supervision, develop strategies in novel environments, and even improve its own performance by identifying weaknesses in its operations and making adjustments. In a sense, it can think and reason across various domains, just as humans can switch between different types of work or adapt to entirely new situations. This level of cognitive flexibility is one of the defining features of General AI.

A key aspect of General AI is its self-improvement capacity. This means that, rather than relying solely on external input and programmed instructions, General AI systems can modify their internal processes based on the information they gather, effectively "learning how to learn." Such systems would be able to process new information, discover patterns, and develop strategies to tackle problems without needing constant reprogramming or retraining. This autonomous evolution is what makes General AI so powerful and potentially transformative across all sectors, from healthcare and education to space exploration and entertainment.

In essence, General AI is not constrained by the narrow capabilities of its predecessors. It has the potential to adapt, evolve, and solve problems across a wide variety of contexts, making it a true leap toward artificial intelligence that can think, reason, and act in ways that are similar to human cognition. The development of such systems remains a goal for AI researchers, though it is still in the early stages, with significant challenges ahead.

DeepMind has been at the forefront of AI research, pushing the boundaries of what artificial intelligence can achieve. Through its innovative projects like Socratic Learning and the Gemini system, the company is paving the way for the eventual realization of General AI—an AI that can autonomously perform a wide range of tasks, adapt to new environments, and continuously improve without human intervention.

At the core of DeepMind's approach is the concept of **Socratic Learning**, which allows AI systems to learn through questioning and self-improvement, much like how humans develop understanding. Unlike traditional AI models that require vast amounts of predefined data and constant human supervision, Socratic Learning allows AI to generate its own learning challenges. It uses a form of recursive learning, where the system actively seeks out gaps in its knowledge and builds upon its existing understanding. This self-sustaining cycle of learning is a key step toward developing more autonomous systems that can evolve without constant input from human trainers. In essence, Socratic Learning mimics the way humans learn and adapt by fostering a system of curiosity and self-improvement.

DeepMind's work with **Gemini**, its multimodal AI system, is another significant leap toward General AI. Gemini represents a shift from traditional, narrowly focused AI to a more flexible, adaptable system that can understand and interact across various media—text, images, audio, and more. By combining these capabilities, Gemini has the potential to understand context more deeply and offer responses or solutions that are not limited to a single domain of knowledge. The ability to integrate multiple forms of input allows Gemini to operate more like a human being, processing complex, multidimensional information in real-time and across a wide range of tasks.

Through these innovations, DeepMind is building the foundation for AI that can learn not just within predefined parameters but across a vast array of scenarios. The move toward self-learning, self-improving systems opens up the possibility for AI to generalize its knowledge, a hallmark of General AI. Rather than being confined to a specific task, these systems will have the potential to tackle a wide variety of challenges in real time, adjusting to new environments and solving problems that they were not specifically trained for.

The implications of these advancements could be profound. If AI systems like those developed by DeepMind continue to evolve and approach true General AI, they could revolutionize nearly every facet of society. In healthcare, for instance, self-learning AI could adapt to new diseases and treatments, offering personalized, real-time medical care. In business, autonomous systems could analyze vast datasets, optimize operations, and predict market trends with incredible accuracy. Even in daily life, these AI systems could provide seamless, intelligent assistance, acting as personalized helpers in everything from home management to education.

The societal changes that could result from the development of truly autonomous, self-improving systems are equally transformative. In the workforce, AI could take over repetitive, time-consuming tasks, freeing up humans to focus on creative and strategic roles. This could lead to significant shifts in job markets, as certain industries may experience automation, while others could thrive with the help of AI. However, this transition will require careful management to ensure that the benefits of AI are distributed equitably and that human workers are not left behind.

Moreover, as AI becomes more autonomous, ethical considerations will take center stage. How do we ensure that these systems align with human values and do not cause harm? What happens when an AI system learns in ways that go beyond our understanding or control? These are questions that must be addressed as AI evolves toward General Intelligence. The challenge will be to ensure that as these systems become more powerful, they remain aligned with human oversight and societal norms.

In conclusion, DeepMind's pioneering work with Socratic Learning and Gemini is laying the groundwork for a future where General AI is not just a theoretical concept but a tangible, practical reality. As these systems evolve, they will not only redefine the role of AI in our lives but also reshape the very fabric of society, challenging our perceptions of intelligence, autonomy, and the future of work. The journey toward General AI is an exciting and daunting one, with the potential to unlock unprecedented technological and societal advancements, but also fraught with complex ethical and practical challenges. The path

DeepMind is carving could very well lead to a future where AI and humanity work together in ways we've never imagined before.

Chapter 9: The Future of AI: Ethical Dilemmas and Societal Impacts

As AI systems become increasingly sophisticated, their ethical implications grow ever more significant. The development of AI is not just a technological endeavor; it is a profound challenge that forces society to confront deep philosophical and moral questions. The drive for more autonomous, self-learning systems raises crucial concerns about fairness, bias, accountability, and control—issues that must be addressed to ensure AI benefits humanity without causing harm.

One of the most pressing ethical concerns is **bias** in AI systems. AI models, especially those built on large datasets, are at risk of reflecting and even amplifying the biases present in those datasets. These biases can stem from a variety of sources: societal inequalities, historical prejudices, or skewed data collection practices. For instance, if an AI system is trained on biased data—such as hiring data that reflects a history of discrimination—there's a real risk that the AI will perpetuate or even exacerbate these biases. In areas like hiring, lending, criminal justice, and healthcare, biased algorithms can lead to unfair outcomes, disproportionately affecting marginalized communities. Addressing this issue requires more than just technical fixes; it demands systemic changes in how data is collected, analyzed, and used in AI training.

Equally troubling is the issue of **fairness**. The question of fairness in AI is complex because fairness can be subjective, varying based on cultural, legal, and societal norms. What one group considers fair might seem unfair to another. As AI systems increasingly make decisions that affect people's lives—such as which applicants are selected for a job or who gets approved for a loan—ensuring these systems operate in a way that is just and equitable becomes a monumental task. Developers must carefully consider how AI systems weigh different factors in decision-making and whether these decisions disproportionately benefit or disadvantage any particular group. This brings us to another significant ethical challenge: **accountability**.

As AI systems become more autonomous, the question of **who is responsible** for their actions becomes increasingly complicated. If an autonomous AI system causes harm, whether through a biased decision, an error, or even an unintended consequence, who is liable? Is it the developers who created the system, the companies deploying it, or the AI itself? In the case of deeply integrated AI systems that evolve and adapt independently, assigning responsibility becomes murky. This is especially concerning in high-stakes areas such as law enforcement, healthcare, and autonomous vehicles, where AI's actions can have life-or-death consequences. Ensuring that there is clear accountability—along with safeguards and oversight mechanisms—is crucial to prevent misuse and to ensure that AI systems are acting in ways that align with human values and ethical standards.

The question of **responsible AI development** becomes even more urgent as AI systems become more capable and autonomous. Traditional models of AI development relied heavily on human oversight, with clear guidelines and boundaries set by developers. However, self-learning AI systems, particularly those based on models like DeepMind's Socratic Learning, are capable of evolving independently. This raises the risk that AI could develop in ways that are unpredictable, or worse, harmful. As AI becomes more autonomous, developers must ensure that there are strong ethical frameworks in place to guide its growth, ensuring that AI systems remain aligned with the values and goals of human society.

One approach to ensuring responsible development is **transparency**. It's critical that AI systems, especially those that are used in decision-making processes, operate in ways that are understandable and traceable. Developers must be able to explain how AI arrived at a particular decision or recommendation, even when the system has been trained to adapt and learn on its own. Without this transparency, it becomes difficult to identify and correct issues such as bias, fairness, or accountability failures. Moreover, ensuring that AI systems are explainable to the public and to regulatory bodies can help mitigate concerns about misuse or exploitation.

Another key consideration is **privacy**. As AI systems gather and process vast amounts of personal data, the risk of privacy violations increases. These systems can track user behavior, analyze interactions, and even predict personal preferences, all of which raise concerns about data security and the potential for surveillance. While AI offers tremendous benefits in fields like healthcare, personalized education, and mental health, it also carries the risk of infringing on individual privacy rights. Balancing the potential for personalized services with the need to protect personal data is an ongoing challenge that requires strict regulatory oversight and the implementation of ethical guidelines for data usage.

Lastly, there is the question of **AI's impact on jobs and society**. As AI becomes more capable, it will likely replace human workers in many industries, leading to significant economic and social disruption. While automation promises to increase efficiency and productivity, it also poses the risk of job displacement for millions of workers, particularly in fields like manufacturing, logistics, and even healthcare. The ethical dilemma here lies in how to manage this transition in a way that minimizes harm to workers and ensures that the benefits of AI are shared broadly. Society must grapple with how to provide retraining opportunities, social safety nets, and new employment options to those whose jobs are at risk due to automation.

In conclusion, the ethical issues surrounding AI development are complex, multifaceted, and increasingly urgent. As AI systems become more autonomous and self-improving, it is essential that we address concerns about bias, fairness, accountability, privacy, and the broader societal implications. This requires not only technical innovation but also a deep commitment to ethical principles and a collaborative effort between developers, policymakers, and the public to ensure that AI is developed and deployed in ways that benefit all of humanity. The road to responsible AI development is challenging, but it is necessary for creating a future where AI enhances, rather than undermines, our shared values and rights.

As the development of advanced AI continues to accelerate, it raises fundamental questions about its potential impact on society. Will AI serve as a powerful ally, enhancing our lives in ways we cannot yet fully comprehend? Or will it pose risks to jobs, privacy, and personal autonomy, reshaping the world in ways that we may not be prepared for? The debate over AI's role in society is complex, with passionate arguments on both sides.

The Case for AI as a Friend

AI's potential to improve lives is immense. In healthcare, for instance, AI-driven systems are already transforming diagnostics, treatment plans, and patient care. Machine learning algorithms can analyze medical data at unprecedented speeds, enabling earlier detection of diseases like cancer, heart disease, and neurological disorders. AI's ability to identify patterns in large datasets can lead to breakthroughs in personalized medicine, helping doctors design treatments tailored specifically to an individual's genetic makeup. Furthermore, AI has the potential to drastically reduce human error in critical fields, improving safety and efficiency.

In education, AI offers opportunities for personalized learning experiences. Intelligent tutoring systems can adapt to the needs of individual students, providing customized lessons and real-time feedback. This not only helps students learn at their own pace but can also make education more accessible to people around the world, regardless of geographical location. AI-driven tools can also help teachers manage administrative tasks, giving them more time to focus on teaching and mentorship.

In business and customer service, AI promises to streamline operations, automate repetitive tasks, and create more personalized experiences for consumers. Virtual assistants, powered by AI, are already helping people manage their daily lives, from scheduling appointments to controlling smart home devices. AI's potential to optimize everything from supply chains to marketing strategies can boost productivity, lower costs, and create new business models that were previously impossible.

Furthermore, AI could offer groundbreaking solutions to some of the world's most pressing challenges. In environmental conservation, AI can help monitor ecosystems, predict climate change, and optimize energy use, contributing to sustainability efforts. In urban planning, AI can improve the efficiency of cities, helping to manage traffic, reduce pollution, and enhance the quality of life for residents.

The Case for AI as a Foe

Despite the many promising applications of AI, there are significant concerns about its societal impact, particularly regarding jobs, privacy, and control.

The most immediate concern is the potential for **job displacement**. As AI systems become more capable of performing tasks traditionally done by humans, many jobs, especially those in manual labor, transportation, and administrative support, could be at risk. For instance, self-driving trucks could replace drivers, while AI-powered software may automate customer service jobs. While automation may lead to new opportunities in tech and AI-related fields, it also raises the fear of widespread unemployment and economic inequality. The workers who are displaced may not have the skills needed to transition into new roles, creating a potential crisis in terms of both employment and social welfare.

Moreover, AI's ability to perform tasks at high speed and with incredible accuracy could lead to increased **economic concentration**. Companies that are at the forefront of AI development could gain significant advantages over smaller businesses and workers, leading to monopolies and widening income inequality. This could exacerbate existing social divides, creating a future where wealth and power are increasingly concentrated in the hands of a few tech giants.

Privacy is another major concern. As AI systems become more integrated into our daily lives, they collect vast amounts of personal data—everything from our online behavior to our medical history. This data is crucial for AI's functionality, but it also opens the door to potential invasions of privacy. While data collection can lead to more personalized services and experiences, it also raises the risk of surveillance, data breaches, and misuse. Governments and corporations could use AI to track individuals' movements, preferences, and actions, undermining privacy rights and even potentially leading to systems of social control.

The issue of **autonomy and control** is perhaps the most unsettling. As AI systems become more autonomous, there is growing concern about who will control these systems and how they will be used. What happens when AI makes decisions that are difficult for humans to understand or challenge? If AI continues to evolve in ways that are not fully predictable or transparent, it could lead to situations where decisions that affect people's lives—such as hiring, law enforcement, and healthcare—are made by systems that are beyond human oversight. This could result in a loss of agency for individuals, as they become subject to the decisions of algorithms that operate without sufficient transparency or accountability.

The fear of **AI surpassing human control** also looms large. As AI becomes more intelligent and autonomous, there are concerns that it could eventually exceed human capabilities, leading to unintended consequences. Some theorists warn that highly autonomous AI systems could act in ways that are not aligned with human values, even if they were designed with the best intentions. This concern, often referred to as the "AI alignment problem," highlights the risks of creating systems that are too powerful to be contained or controlled.

A Balanced Perspective

While it is clear that AI presents both opportunities and challenges, the key to ensuring that it benefits society lies in how it is developed, regulated, and integrated into our lives. **Ethical AI development** must be a priority, ensuring that AI systems are transparent, fair, and accountable.

Developers must actively work to mitigate biases in algorithms, protect privacy, and prevent misuse of AI technologies.

Moreover, society needs to prepare for the potential social and economic disruption caused by AI. This includes creating **new educational opportunities**, fostering a culture of lifelong learning, and rethinking the nature of work in an increasingly automated world. Governments and organizations must work together to ensure that AI's benefits are distributed equitably and that safeguards are in place to protect the most vulnerable.

Ultimately, whether AI becomes a friend or foe depends on the choices we make today. By prioritizing ethics, fairness, and transparency, and by working to ensure that AI complements human capabilities rather than replacing them, we can shape a future where AI enhances our lives rather than threatening our freedoms. The path forward is not predetermined, but it is in our hands.

Conclusion

As we stand on the precipice of a new era in artificial intelligence, the advancements we've witnessed thus far only hint at the potential that lies ahead. From the early days of rule-based systems to the revolutionary breakthroughs in machine learning, reinforcement learning, and DeepMind's Socratic Learning, the trajectory of AI has been nothing short of extraordinary. The development of multimodal systems like Gemini, which combine text, images, and audio processing, showcases AI's increasing versatility and its ability to integrate more seamlessly into the fabric of human life. AI is no longer just a tool that performs tasks; it is evolving into an entity capable of understanding, learning, and even forming personal connections with humans.

Looking forward, the trajectory of AI technology seems poised for even greater milestones. As systems like Gemini and Socratic Learning continue to evolve, we can expect AI to not only become more autonomous but also more adaptive, allowing it to respond to complex, ever-changing environments. The potential for AI to solve some of the world's most pressing issues—whether it's in healthcare, climate change, or the global economy—remains a powerful motivator for further development. AI's ability to analyze vast amounts of data at unprecedented speeds could lead to breakthroughs in nearly every field, from diagnostics and treatment in medicine to optimized urban planning and environmental conservation.

But as AI continues to grow in power and scope, it is essential that we navigate this new world with caution. Responsible development will be crucial in ensuring that AI systems are designed ethically and with a keen awareness of their social, economic, and political implications. This means embedding transparency, fairness, and accountability into AI systems, preventing biases from creeping into the algorithms that influence our lives. It also means creating regulatory frameworks that safeguard privacy and human rights while encouraging innovation. The future of AI must not be driven by a race to develop the most powerful systems but by a collective commitment to harnessing AI's capabilities in ways that benefit all of humanity.

Equally important is the collaboration between humans and machines. Rather than viewing AI as a replacement for human workers or a threat to personal freedoms, we must embrace AI as a partner—one that can augment human capabilities and improve our lives in ways we have yet to fully understand. AI has the potential to revolutionize industries and create new opportunities for people around the world. But this future can only be realized if we approach AI development with a sense of responsibility, foresight, and an unwavering commitment to making the world a better place for all.

The role AI will play in shaping the future of humanity, technology, and society is both exciting and daunting. As we move further into the age of artificial intelligence, the choices we make today will have far-reaching consequences. Will AI become a force for good, enhancing human life and addressing the challenges we face as a global community? Or will it become a tool of control, surveillance, and division? The future is unwritten, but one thing is certain: AI is here to stay, and how we choose to integrate it into our lives will define the next chapter of our collective history.

In the end, the question is not whether AI will reshape our world—it's how we will shape AI to ensure it serves the greater good. As we continue to unlock the potential of machine intelligence, we must do so with the knowledge that AI's impact on society, for better or worse, is in our hands. Let us approach the future of AI with a vision that is both ambitious and responsible, for the decisions we make today will echo in the technological landscape of tomorrow.

www.ingramcontent.com/pod-product-compliance
Lightning Source LLC
LaVergne TN
LVHW022354060326
832902LV00022B/4436